A Vindication of the Continued Succession of the Primitive Church of Jesus Christ

(Now Scandalously Termed Anabaptists)
From The Apostles Unto This Present Time

Published by
John Spittlehouse and John More
London: 1652

Edited
With an Introduction
by
Gery Schmidt

Published by
Providence Strict Baptist Assembly
203-1138 Yates Street
Victoria, British Columbia
V8V 3M8
2001

104

A
VINDICATION
OF THE
Continued Succeſsion of the Primitive Church of Jeſus Chriſt (now ſcandalouſly termed Anabaptiſts) from the Apoſtles unto this preſent time.

In Anſwer to three following Aſſertions, Extracted out of the Writings of Mr. *John Brain*, and chiefly out of his Book, Intituled,

The Churches going in, and coming out of the Wilderneſs, Viz.

1. *That the Goſpel-frame of the Primitive Church hath been devolved into the Antichriſtian Eſtate, and condition, ſince from about the year* 406. *unto this preſent time.*
2. *That during the aforeſaid time, there hath not been a true Church-frame of Goſpel-government.*
3. *That the Goſpel-frame of the Goſpel-government, is to be reſtored again by ſome one Man, who ſhall have Authoritie given him from above, to reſtore Baptiſm, and all other loſt Ordinances of the Church.*

And may alſo ſerve as a further Caveat, to the preſent deluded People of this Nation, that are yet ſeduced by the crafty *Demetriouſſes* of the Times, who for love of Gain, ſtill indeavour to cry up their *Diana* of *Rome* whom *England*, and all they call Chriſtendome yet Worſhip.

MATTH. 28. 19, 20. *Goe yee therefore and teach all Nations baptizing them*, &c. *Teaching them to obſerve all things*, &c. *And loe I am with you alwayes, even unto the end of the World*, Amen.

JOHN 10. 1. 7, 8, 9, 10, 16.

Publiſhed by *John Spittlehouſe*, and *John More*.

London, Printed by *Gartrude Dawſon*, 1652.

Introduction

I The Tract and Its Publishers

The present tract before the reader is an exceedingly rare one indeed. According to David Wing's *Short-Title Catalogue 1641-1700*, only one copy of Spittlehouse and More's *Vindication* is known to be extant in any library in the world. And this copy resides at the American Baptist Historical Society in Rochester, New York (who, incidentally, kindly furnished me with an excellent photo-copy of the original). It is not even listed in W.T. Whitley's *A Baptist Bibliography* which was published in England in 1916. But this tract not only suffers from extreme scarcity, it also suffers (alas) from the defect of missing pages. Of the original thirty pages of text, four pages (i.e. pp. 17-20) are wanting. This defect, however, does not render useless the republishing of Spittlehouse and More's work. Indeed, as it will be seen shortly, the republishing of this work, defective though it be, is important not only from a theological standpoint, but especially from a historical one. Though only one copy is at present *known* to exist in the world, there is the possibility of other copies existing (complete with missing pages), whether bound up in the midst of other pamphlets, or which may reside in someone's private library. At any rate, the present republication of this tract represents an endeavour by God's grace to render this work rare no more.

In terms of theme, this aspect of the tract is clearly manifest in the very title of the work. Messrs. Spittlehouse and More laboured to defend the doctrine of the perpetuity of Christ's assembly. And the kind of *ekklesia* they argue is perpetual is not the ecclesiastical nonentity that we have come to know through theological history as the universal invisible church, but rather a local congregation of immersed disciples who follow Christ and keep his commands. This work was also produced in a particular polemical context. It was written in response to the assertions found in the writings of a certain John Brain (also spelled Brayne), and in particular to a work of his entitled *The Church's Going In, and Coming Out of The Wilderness* (published in 1649). There are three points (as seen in the title page) that Spittlehouse and More seek to refute in Brain's work. First, that the "gospel-frame of the primitive church" disappeared from the earth in A.D. 406 by being absorbed, or "devolved," into the "Antichristian Estate." Second, that from A.D. 406 to 1649 (the year Brain's book was published) there had been no "true church-frame of gospel-government;" and third, that the true "gospel-frame of the gospel-government," along with all lost ordinances (including baptism), was to be restored by some man having "authority given him from above." Both Spittlehouse and More argue that Christ's assembly, with its frame, government, and ordinances, had always existed on earth, though owing to persecution, often in a hidden state; and consequently, there was no need to restore what had never been lost in the first place.

In considering next the character of the *Vindication*, one specific element demands our attention. For too long now both proponents and opponents of assembly perpetuity have erroneously sought to build their respective cases upon a purely *historical* foundation as opposed to a *Scriptural* one. Spittlehouse and More, though they do not avoid history outright, nonetheless found their argument on the Scriptures. And as the reader will soon discover, Revelation 12:6 represents the textual backbone of the tract. Whether one agrees with their exegesis or not, Spittlehouse and More certainly approach the subject of church perpetuity from the only viable standpoint a Christian should take, namely, God's infallible and inerrant word. They pursue neither the scientific/empirical "seeing is believing" method of the scientific Baptist, nor the historical chain-link method of the modern Landmarker. They are content to rest their case on the foundation of God's word.

With respect to the publishers/authors of this tract, very little is known about John Spittlehouse and John More. Relative to the latter, Whitley lists six works by More ranging in date from 1652 to 1670. One work in particular, namely, *A General Exhortation To The World* (published in 1652) is actually advertized at the end of the *Vindication*. Aside from this, the only other information on More I have been able to gather is the following, also found in Whitley's *Baptist Bibliography*: "relation of Spittlehouse; trustee for Joseph Davies 1700-1; died 1701-2" (vol. 1, p. 224). With respect to John Spittlehouse, Whitley lists some sixteen works by this individual dating from 1649 to 1658 (vol. l, p. 228). He is listed among the ranks of Seventh Day Baptists (not to be confounded with the cult of Seventh Day Adventists) by historian Don Sanford in his work *A Choosing People: The History of Seventh Day Baptists*. Owing to scarcity of materials, Sanford can do little more than mention his name all of three times.

In the *Dictionary of National Biography*, a short paragraph appears on Spittlehouse, the greater part of which is now quoted for the reader's information:

> Pamphleteer, fought for the parliament against the king at Gainsborough and at the siege of Newark (1644), remaining in the army till after the battle of Worcester (1651) (*Cal. State Papers*, Dom. 1654, p. 62). When Cromwell dissolved the Long Parliament (20 April 1653), Spittlehouse published several pamphlets in defence of that action, and urged that Cromwell should imitate Moses in appointing governors for the people. On 5 Dec. 1653 the sergeant-

at-arms was ordered to apprehend him and bring him before council to answer for certain petitions presented by him to council and parliament (ib. 1653-4, pp. 272, 294, 446). He was released by order of council on 6 April 1654, but his arrest was again directed on 19 Oct. for publishing an abusive answer to Cromwell's speech of 4 Sept. 1654 (ib. 1654, pp. 378, 434). His release, on giving a bond to the extent of 200 l. to live peaceably was voted on 1 Feb. 1656 (ib. 1655-6, p. 155). The date of his death is not known (vol. 18, p. 814).

II Purpose For Republishing The *Vindication*

The doctrine of church perpetuity is often perceived and portrayed among Baptists as the nineteenth-century offspring of what has become known as Landmarkism. In particular, the names of J.M. Pendleton (1811-1891), A.C. Dayton (1813-1865), and J.R. Graves (1820-1893) are ever associated with the formation and popularizing of Landmark views. Relative to the perpetuity of Christ's congregation, as developed and maintained by these men, many non-successionist Baptist historians have asserted that prior to the nineteenth century no Baptist held to, or advocated, such views as espoused by Pendleton, Dayton, and Graves. The following statement by W. Morgan Patterson, from his small work entitled, *Baptist Successionism A Critical View*, represents a classic example of such an attitude:

> The Baptist spirit of the seventeenth century was opposed to the mechanical succession concept. There is evidence of a feeling of spiritual consanguinity to preceding generations of Christians, as all were related in the "invisible church" (a term often found), but apologies for any kind of succession of Baptist churches as advocated in the nineteenth and twentieth centuries are nonexistent (pp. 18, 19).

Now it is statements like this that serve as the impetus for the republishing of Spittlehouse and More's *Vindication*. The very existence of such a tract, published well over a century before Pendleton, Dayton, and Graves first saw the light of day, demonstrates the utterly erroneous and misleading character of Patterson's statement. But not only does the *Vindication* prove church perpetuity was believed and defended by Baptists prior to the nineteenth century, a careful perusal of this work also reveals that the very mode of argumentation employed by Spittlehouse and More remarkably parallels that to be found in later Landmark literature. Let us consider the following examples comparing the *Vindication* to statements culled from J.R. Graves' two works entitled *Tri-lemma* and *Old Landmarkism - What Is It?*

The first example relates to how Spittlehouse, More, and Graves ultimately rested their respective cases for assembly perpetuity on a Scriptural foundation, as opposed to a historical one. In the *Vindication*, the following occurs:

> Object. Peradventure you will bid me prove that the aforesaid primitive church was so preserved, and where. Answ. It is enough for me to prove that it was only to be hid, and so hid from the face of the Dragon &c. (p. 30; pagination from the original).

This statement clearly reflects a state of contentedness to fully rest the case for church perpetuity on Scripture (in this particular case, Rev. 12:6), as opposed to history. The same is to be seen in the following statement from Graves' *Old Landmarkism - What Is It?*

> We do not admit that it devolves upon us more than upon every other lover of Jesus to prove, by incontestible historical facts that this kingdom of the Messiah has stood from the day it was set up by Him, unbroken and unmoved; to question it, is to doubt His sure word of promise (p. 84).

The next example demonstrates that Spittlehouse, More, and Graves interpreted Revelation 12:6 in precisely the same manner. The *Vindication* states the following:

> Again, it is as plain from Scripture, where it is said "That the manchild, who was to rule all nations with a rod of iron, was caught up unto God, and to his throne;" as also that the woman "fled into the wilderness, where she had a place prepared of God, wherein she should be fed a thousand two hundred and threescore days," Rev. 12. 5, 6. But antichrist, or the Papacy of Rome, &c. was neither the place, where the aforesaid woman, and her manchild (viz. the primitive church and her frame of government) was either to be caught up or fed... (pp. 3, 4).

The following statements of Graves come respectively from Old *Landmarkism* and *Tri-lemma*:

> And the woman [church of Christ] fled into the wilderness [obscurity] where she hath a place prepared by God, that there they may nourish her a thousand two hundred and sixty days [each day for a year] - Rev. 12:6 (p. 111).

> They claim (i.e. Baptists - ed.) that they can trace the history of communities, essentially like themselves, back through the "wilderness," into which they were driven by the dragon... (p. 119).

A third example illustrates clearly how both parties were convinced that Protestants are but children of the Papacy, and hence, the daughters of Rome (i.e. the Harlot). First, the *Vindication*:

> ... therefore the Papists may boldly, and justly, question the Prelates, where their religion was before Luther, as also the Presbyterians before Calvin, inasmuch they are no other than the daughters of that grand Harlot, Rev. 17. 5. Witness their national churches, their Popish institution of priests, and baptizing of infants, which are infallible characters, to prove them harlots like their mother (p. 15).

Next, Graves' *Tri-lemma*:

> Could not Rome thus cause the well-aimed blow to recoil upon her Protestant children, for they are her legitimate offspring; and if she is the mother of abominations and harlots, Protestants are they (pp. 82, 83).

Fourthly, Spittlehouse, More, and Graves all saw the clear ecclesiastical connection between Rome and Protestantism, since the latter received their sprinklings/ordinations from the former, and hence that Protestant ecclesiology as a whole was thereby null and void. Consider the following lengthy extract from the *Vindication*:

> Now they (i.e. Protestants - ed.) cannot avoid but that the constitution of their church, is now the same with that party, or church, which did separate from the Papacy of that time, from which they derive their succession (p. 21).
>
> ... that all such persons as have been incorporated into church-fellowship by being baptized or sprinkled, while infants were incorporated by a way or means that Jesus Christ never commanded to be used to such a purpose, as also by such a way as was never practiced by his apostles, and so consequently not incorporated visible members of the church of Jesus Christ, but contrariwise, visible members of the visible church of antichrist, whose invention it was, and whose practice it yet is, instance Mr. Cranford's church as aforesaid, and therefore as antichristian as the rest; and so consequently the ordination, which Mr. Cranford and the rest of the ministers of London (Presbyterian ministers) have received, from such as have been so baptized or sprinkled as aforesaid, is every whit as antichristian as their baptism, which hath been abominable in the church of Jesus Christ, Mat. 15. 8. Having thus clearly proved, that all the aforesaid societies of people, are neither churches or ministers of Jesus Christ (albeit their separations as aforesaid)... (p. 27).

Now compare Graves' testimony from his *Tri-lemma*:

> The Presbyterian General Assembly not able to decide this question: "Is baptism in the Romish Church valid?" affirmatively or negatively without unbaptizing and unchurching the whole Protestant world! (from the title page).

> That Presbyterians, in common with all the Reformed or Protestant sects, received their baptisms and ordinations from the Romish apostasy, is denied by no one, is admitted by the Assembly itself (p. 26).
>
> How can Baptists deny the validity of the ordinances of the Romish Church, without thereby destroying Protestant baptisms and ordinations? (p. 89).

These preceding examples (which can be easily greatly multiplied) clearly demonstrate the similarity of reasoning between Spittlehouse, More, and Graves. And they are of such a character that cannot be regarded as superficial in nature. Indeed, such Baptists who are already familiar with the writings of J.R. Graves will in many ways feel that in reading the *Vindication* they are simply reading Graves from a seventeenth-century standpoint. Non-successionist Baptist historians, who prefer to found their arguments on history rather than on the Bible, have been guilty of misleading Baptists on the question of church perpetuity for over a century now. It is hoped that in republishing Spittlehouse and More's *Vindication* such may possess enough honesty to retract the erroneous statements that have been made in regard to pre-nineteenth century Baptist sentiments concerning church perpetuity.

III The Editorial Process

Relative to editing, I have sought to be as simple as possible, and therefore, to change as little as possible. In terms of the text, it is essentially unchanged, save that many words have been updated in spelling, some capital letters reduced to smaller case, and the odd punctuation change made. I have also eliminated in many instances what I consider to be an excessive use of italics, by either rendering the text within quotation marks, or simply in regular typeface. The only significant editorial change made is that I have reduced all the marginal notes to footnotes, with consecutive enumeration as opposed to the threefold use of symbol, letter, and number in the original. It is hoped that the editorial process employed will make this valuable tract readable to a new generation of readers.

Gery Schmidt

Providence Strict Baptist

Assembly, Victoria, B.C.

September 17, 2001

A VINDICATION OF THE Continued Succession of the Primitive Church of Jesus Christ (now scandalously termed Anabaptists) from the Apostles unto this present time.

In Answer to three following Assertions, Extracted out of the Writings of Mr. John Brain, and chiefly out of his Book, Intituled,

The Churches going in, and coming out of the Wilderness, Viz.

1. That the Gospel-frame of the Primitive Church hath been devolved into the Antichristian Estate, and condition, since from about the year 406. unto this present time.
2. That during the aforesaid time, there hath not been a true Church-frame of Gospel-government.
3. That the Gospel-frame of the Gospel-government, is to be restored again by some one Man, who shall have Authoritie given him from above, to restore Baptism, and all other lost Ordinances of the Church.

And may also serve as a further Caveat, to the present deluded People of this Nation, that are yet seduced by the crasy Demetriousses of the Times, who for love of Gain, still indeavour to cry up their Diana of Rome whom England, and all they call Christendome yet Worship.

MATTH. 28. 19,20. Goe yee therefore and teach all Nations baptizing them, &c. Teaching them to observe all things, &c. And loe I am with you alwayes, even unto the end of the World, Amen.
JOHN 10. 1,7,8,9,10,16.

Published by John Spittlehouse, and John More.

London, Printed by Gartrude Dawson, 1652.

A Vindication of the Continued Succession of The Primitive Church of Jesus Christ (now scandalously termed Anabaptists) from the Apostles unto this present time.

Sir,

Having several times conferred with you about your judgment in the aforesaid particulars, and perceiving your resolution to persevere in them your opinions, I have now undertaken by the power of Jesus Christ, to vindicate a continued succession of his church and ordinances (as aforesaid) against your assertions.

In the first place, I shall declare your meaning by the gospel-frame of gospel-government, (viz. "The true public worship of God, consisting in external ordinances, as of baptism," &c.) which you say hath ceased in the nations this 1200 years, doth yet cease, and shall so cease, until the sanctuary be cleansed.

Having thus explained your meaning, as in relation to the aforesaid frame of gospel-government, I shall in the next place answer to your first assertion, (viz.)

"That the gospel-frame of the primitive church hath been devolved into the antichristian estate, since from about the year 406 to this present time."

In answer to which, I shall oppose your own expressions, in your aforementioned book, hoping such a confutation will be most prevalent with you.

1. I shall begin with that in page 14, where you say, "That Christ and antichrist cannot agree."

But if the aforesaid gospel-frame, &c. had been devolved or mixed with the antichristian frame of worship since the year aforesaid, then they must of necessity have had such a communion and fellowship together, as to become one and the same with each other, (during the aforesaid time) which the aforesaid words do plainly contradict.

Therefore it may be concluded from the aforesaid words, that the aforesaid gospel-frame, &c. was never so devolved or mixed together, as in that your assertion.

2. Again page 2, you acknowledge the aforesaid gospel-frame &c. was to be hid, "and so hid from the face of the Dragon, as that the Dragon could not find it, or make discovery of it."

Now all rational men know, that that which was hid from the Dragon, was neither hid by the Dragon, nor in the Dragon, nor can it be imagined that any one will fly into the bosom of him that seeketh his destruction for sanctuary, which the aforesaid gospel-frame must have done according to your assertion.

3. Again page 2, you also say that the "twelve hundred and sixty days, prophetically years, do clearly show the time of the church's hiding, in its obscure condition, in which time it should not be known unto antichrist, what her estate was."

But antichrist could not be ignorant of the aforesaid gospel-frame, &c. if it had (during the aforesaid time) been devolved, or made one and the same with the aforesaid antichristian frame, &c. For certainly, if so, either must antichrist be ignorant of his own frame, &c. or he must of necessity know the church's: but you have there positively affirmed, that antichrist was not to be acquainted with the primitive church condition during the aforesaid time.

Therefore the gospel-frame of the primitive church during the aforesaid time, had a secret and obscure condition which antichrist, or the men of the world became ignorant of.

4. Again in page 2, you likewise acknowledge the aforesaid gospel-frame to be carried away from the world and antichrist, "as it were into another world, during the aforesaid time, alluding it (in its then condition) to the absence of the sun from us, when it is departed out of our horizon."

But as it is most certain that the sun doth neither cease to shine, or be a sun, while it remaineth so obscure, as aforesaid, or by any other interposition, whatsoever which for a time may cause a seeming appearance to the contrary.

So likewise albeit the aforesaid gospel-frame, &c. hath for so long a time been interposed by Papacy, Prelacy, Presbytery, &c. by reason whereof it hath been totally eclipsed to the world, &c.

Yet certainly as the Israelites could have told the Egyptians that the gross darkness in Egypt, was no prejudice to them in Goshen, so likewise hath not the overshadowings of truth by the aforesaid errors, been any prejudice to the true Israel of God while they were in their wilderness, or hidden condition as aforesaid, which in effect you yourself have confessed, page 9, where you acknowledge (by way of simile to what I have said) "That the Israelites in time of their persecution, had light in their dwellings when their persecutors were under darkness:" As also "that God would ever keep and teach us to keep a difference between the godly and ungodly in this," (viz. of Christ from antichrist, truth from error, light from darkness) "as in other divisions made of God." As Israel had the bright side, and the Egyptians the dark side of the cloud towards them; all which doth clearly contradict your aforesaid assertion, for by it you would have all the aforesaid gospel-frame, &c. so confounded together with that of antichrist's, as to become one with each other, making an absolute concord and harmony between truth and error, light and darkness, Christ and antichrist.

Again, it is as plain from Scripture, where it is said, "That the manchild, who was to rule all nations with a rod of iron, was caught up unto God, and to his throne;" as also that the woman "fled into the wilderness, where she had a place prepared of God, wherein she should be fed a thousand two hundred and threescore days," Rev. 12. 5,6.

But antichrist, or the Papacy of Rome, &c. was neither the place where the aforesaid woman, and her manchild (viz. the primitive church and her frame of government) was either to be caught up or fed, unless you will make the seat of the Papacy the throne of God, and antichrist and his consort (the Mother of Harlots) their foster-father and mother, during the aforesaid time, which cannot be.

First, in that the aforesaid manchild is said to be caught up "unto God," and to his throne, as in point of safety and preservation, from the fury and rage of the Dragon, &c.

But antichrist did not any ways preserve the primitive church, or its frame of government, but contrariwise hath endeavoured to subvert it.

Therefore the aforesaid antichrist and his consort, did not any ways preserve the aforesaid manchild from their own fury against it, neither is it rational to imagine they would, in that its ruin was to become the other's rise.

Secondly, because the woman, &c. is said to flee into the wilderness, &c. where she should be fed, &c.

But that antichrist, and his aforesaid consort, should preserve the primitive church in its purity (for otherwise how is it preserved) is contrary to common sense, for the reasons aforesaid. Or that they should feed it with primitive truths in relation to its essentials, substantials, and circumstantials, (for otherwise how could it be truly fed) which is every whit as contrary to common sense that they would. And that for the aforesaid reason. Therefore it is also as impossible that the aforesaid antichrist, &c. did either preserve, or feed the aforesaid primitive church, &c. in its aforesaid wilderness condition.

Yea, you yourself have acknowledged, "That Jerusalem and Babel, have their ordinances and worships so distinct one from the other, that what is of and in the one, is not of, nor cannot be in the other." And if so, then how is it that you should so confound them together? &c.

Object. I know you will produce Dr. Taylor in his tract, &c. against this, where he saith, "That the church's flight was not in respect of motion, but of state and condition, not a change of place but condition,"

&c. For which expressions you seem very highly to applaud him.

But before you too highly exalt him for that saying, I desire to know by what logic either that doctor, or yourself, can prove the flight of anything without motion or change of place: As for his instance in point of condition I assent so far unto, as that the primitive church, &c. was brought unto an exceeding great outward hardship, through the tyranny of that man of sin, and his adherents.

Again, if the antichristian frame aforesaid, was intended by God to be the wilderness, in which the aforesaid primitive church, &c. was to be hid, &c. then it must also of necessity come out of the said antichristian wilderness again, as the title of your aforesaid book attesteth.

And if so, then Prelacy, Presbytery, &c. have been Christian conversions, which elsewhere you utterly deny, where you say, the way of worship which proceedeth from Rome must cease, and that it is not the way of propagating the gospel, as also, that God will not be found in it, and if so, how shall the true church-frame, &c. be found in it? And if it be not in it, it cannot be extracted out of it, for if so, then a clean thing may be brought out of an unclean, contrary to that of Job 14. 4 and James 3. 11,12. You likewise term the reformings aforesaid, to be the reformings of Rome, or Babel, &c. (and not of Christ) as indeed they are.

By all which it doth clearly appear, that the primitive church, &c. was not devolved, or mixed with the aforesaid antichristian frame during the time aforesaid, and that from your own expressions.

I shall now proceed to your second argument, viz. "That during the aforesaid time, there hath not been a true church-frame," &c.

Object. In confirmation of which, you cite Hilary of Poitiers in France, who lived in the year 380 and saith, "That in his days the primitive church was not to be found in houses, in temples, or cities, but in prisons, mountains, dens, deserts, and caves of the earth."

Answ. Now I appeal to any rational man, whether that historian hath in so saying proved the aforesaid primitive church to have been without a being in that time, but rather to have had a being, albeit in the aforesaid "prisons, mountains, dens, deserts, and caves of the earth," where he concludeth it had then its residence.

Object. Again, albeit the same author saith, "That in the 26th year after, there was a more exceeding increase of darkness, than in the time before."

Answ. Yet that proveth no more a darkness in reference to the aforesaid primitive, or true church, than the absence of the sun from us in England, doth prove the like to all the habitable earth at the same time, so that albeit the splendor of that gospel-mercy (as you term it) was then withdrawn from the view of antichrist, &c. for the time aforesaid, yet certainly it did retain its lustre in itself, for it is every whit as possible to separate the light from the body of the sun, as it was possible for antichrist to separate the gospel-frame, &c. from the body of the true church of Jesus Christ.

Object. You will say, "Where was there any one visible society of saints, which did practice according to the apostles' rules and precepts?"

Answ. The not-appearance of a visible body or society of saints to the public view of antichrist, &c. doth no more prove, that the true church had no visible estate in itself, than the sun ceaseth to be a sun, during the absence of the light thereof; neither is it more to be imagined, that the true church, during its hidden, or wilderness condition, did desist from practicing according to the apostles' rules, and precepts, (so far as the well-being of such small societies did require) than it is to imagine, that there was not two or three saints left living upon the face of the earth, which I suppose you will not affirm.

Object. You will say, "Antichrist was to take his rise, by taking down the gospel-frame of gospel-government, making that to be hid, that he might only appear."

Answ. His rise was not by taking down the gospel-frame, &c. *but by setting up another frame of his own, apart from it, and contrary unto it,* as is also confessed by you (as in pag. 10) where you say, he took his rise "by setting up a counterfeit way of his own, carrying a false light with it by which he bewitched the nations with the cup of abominations, deceiving poor silly souls with the outward show of religion and piety," &c. by which expressions you have proved for me that antichrist was not to take his rise by taking down the gospel-frame, &c. according to your aforesaid assertions.

Object. But I know you will further object, "That the holy city was to be trodden under foot, (which, say you, is meant of the gospel-frame, &c.) and truth by him was to be cast down to the ground, and antichrist was only to prosper," Dan. 8. 12,13. Rev. 11. 2 and 13. 1.

Answ. As it is possible for a man to be cast down to the ground, and also trodden under foot of his enemy, and yet retain life and motion, yea and in time so recover his strength, as to vanquish the vanquisher, as many times it hath happened, and may happen.

So likewise was it as possible for the church of Christ, after her hidden and wilderness condition, to gather such strength and vigour, as to return a double proportion of affliction and misery upon the head of her persecutor, to what she had formerly received of him, and his adherents. As in Revel. 18. vers. 6,7.

Again, as it is impossible that truth in itself should be destroyed by error, so likewise was it also as impossible, that the faith and practice of the then saints, should be destroyed in them, by the antichristian power then predominant over their bodies. Or, that they should become proselytes to his aforesaid delusions. For if the sons of Jonadab, &c. would not transgress the command of their father in the flesh (Jer. cap. 35) how much more is it to be thought that the other would obey the Father of their spirits, in observing of all his precepts which was given them in charge to keep.

Yea the contrary cannot be imagined, unless you will maintain a falling away from grace by the elect, which I know you abominate. Yea the Scriptures do clearly manifest the contrary, by distinguishing of such as were so to be overpowered and deluded by antichrist, by these phrases (viz.) "Such as were to perish," as in 2 Thes. 2. 9,10. "Of such as were not written in the Lamb's book of life," Revel. 13. 8. Yea you acknowledge as much yourself, in your aforesaid expressions, where you term them "silly souls," &c. pag. 10. &c.

So that I may safely conclude, both from the aforenamed Scriptures, and yourself, that antichrist was to prevail over none but such as aforementioned, and if so, then he was not to conquer or subvert the faith and practice of the then saints, and so consequently of none of their successors, who are concluded by the apostle, "To be wise unto salvation," 2 Tim. 3. 15. Yea Christ himself giveth this character of them, "That they will not follow strangers," John 10. 5. &c. as also, "That they know not the voice of strangers," but contrariwise, "that they know his voice, and follow him only," vers. 27. Yea he is said to take such care and cognizance of them, as that "he knoweth them by name," vers. 3. Yea, God the Father is said so to protect them, "as that they shall never perish." Yea, to have so fast hold of them, as that neither man nor devil can pluck them out of his hands, "For that he is more great and powerful than all their adversaries," vers. 29.

It is therefore without all controversy, that antichrist was not to beguile the aforesaid saints of their faith, or to gain them as proselytes to his kingdom of darkness, and so consequently not from the fruits thereof, (viz.) in point of worship, or any precept or command of Jesus Christ whatsoever. The uttermost extent of the power of antichrist consisting only *in persecuting or killing their bodies,* but not to touch their *faith, the life of their souls:* And if not their faith, then not their obedience, which is ever individually annexed unto it as an inseparable consequence thereof.

So that the aforementioned texts in Daniel and the Revelations, must of necessity be understood of the despicable and contemptible estate and condition of the aforesaid saints in the esteem of antichrist, &c. during the time they were to lord it over them, but so far were they from extinguishing or rooting up their faith and obedience to the commands of Christ and his apostles, as that they increased the more in strength by such cruelties, their blood being the seed of the church, as historians do declare of them.

Object. You cite also Mr. Bernard on Rev. 12. 6, "who understands by the church's flight into the wilderness, that she lost her visibility before her enemies."

Answ. I do freely acknowledge as much, but that doth not prove the primitive church was to be unchurched by her enemies in her distressed or wilderness condition, or that she was invisible to such of whom she then consisted, but rather that she was preserved by that her flight from the fury and rage of antichrist.

Object. You cite also Mr. Cooper Bishop of Galloway, who compareth the then hiding of the primitive church and frame of gospel-government unto the hiding of the Popish Church or synagogue in England, "who are (saith he) without public state or regiment, or open free exercise of holy function," &c. Than which expression you think nothing can more fitly and fully clear your aforesaid assertion.

I do likewise freely acknowledge that his expression to be very pertinent to the setting forth of the state of the primitive church under the persecution of antichrist, &c. but little to that purpose you drive at, viz. as to a cessation of the aforesaid primitive church, &c. in that her condition. Yea so far was it from tending to such a construction, as that it doth rather argue the quite contrary, viz. To prove a succession or continuance of the aforesaid primitive church, &c. in that her condition. In prosecution of which we may compare the present estate and condition of the aforesaid Romish Church or regiment in this nation with the other, which if without public state or regiment, &c. in that Bishop's days, certainly much more at this present time, as all rational men must needs acknowledge.

And yet notwithstanding the present restriction by virtue of the Acts now in force against Popish priests and Jesuits, &c. I presume all rational men will acknowledge, that they cannot but conceive and believe that the Popish religion is yet put in practice in this nation, albeit not to the public view of such as will call them in question for so doing.

And if so, then I appeal to any rational man, whether or no the like practice might not have been used by the primitive Christians and their successors, during their persecution by antichrist. Yea, that it was more probable may thus appear. For by how much the aforesaid Papists, &c. dare now be so bold as to support an error; by so much or more may we justly conceive the other would be as valiant to maintain a truth, by practicing what was their duties as members of the true primitive church, yea, I would gladly know any one ordinance of Jesus Christ, that was impossible to be practiced by them (that was requisite to their then present condition) during their enemies' hottest rage against them. Having thus clearly proved a continuation of the primitive church and frame of gospel-government (so far as was requisite for their then present condition) I shall in the next place by the same assistance prove the first approach of its visibility into the world, after its aforesaid persecution under the Dragon and the beast mentioned, Rev. chap. 12 and 13.

And first of its persecution under the aforesaid red Dragon, whose original I take to be the emperor Nero, and that for these ensuing reasons, viz.

In that it is reported of him by Eusebius (lib. 2 ch. 24, 25, fol. 34), "That when he had reigned for the space of 8 years, &c. and being settled in his throne, he fell into abominable facts, and took armour against the service due unto the universal and almighty God, &c. How detestable he was become, is not for this present time to declare, for there be many that have painted out his willful malice, which may easily appear if we consider the furious madness of that man, through the which after that beyond reason he had destroyed an innumerable company, he fell into such a sucking way of slaughter, that he abstained not from his most dear and familiar friends; yea, he tormented with divers kinds of deaths his own mother, his brethren, his wife, and many of his dear kinsfolks, as if they had been enemies, and deadly foes unto him."

Again, it behooved us to take notice of this one thing of him above the rest, viz. "That he was counted the *first enemy* of all the emperors unto the service of God," by which we may conclude, that Nero was the first that began the persecution in the Gentile church of Christ.[1]

Again, Tertullian the Roman writeth thus of the said Nero, viz. "Read your authors, there you shall find Nero chiefly to have persecuted this doctrine at Rome, &c. he became cruel unto all," &c.

Again he saith, "This enemy of God set up himself to the destruction of the apostles, wherein he was first discovered. For they write that Paul was beheaded of him at Rome," &c. all which being compared with Philip. 4. 22 doth clearly demonstrate that they were Paul's followers that were so persecuted by Nero in Rome.[2] Yea, it is very probable, that Nero himself for the first eight years of his reign, did favour Paul's doctrine, or otherwise he would not have suffered so many of his family to have been his followers, as it plainly appears in the aforesaid chapter:

[1]Nero began the first persecution in the Gentile church.

[2]Nero first discovered by acting against Paul.

as also by their aforesaid sufferings by Nero, as the aforesaid histories do relate.

Having thus found out the original of the aforesaid red Dragon, and also the very year wherein he began his persecution, as also in all probability, the first martyr of the Gentile church of Christ, which I take to be the apostle Paul, and that for these reasons, viz.

1. In that he was designed to be the apostle of the Gentiles (Gal. 2. 8,9) it was therefore most requisite, that he should be the first martyr that should suffer under that heathen Dragon, to the end he might as well be their captain in sufferings, as in the practice of the truth which he had taught them, and that according to the example of his Master Jesus Christ.

2. In that the aforesaid tyrant is said to be first discovered by his causing Paul to be beheaded.

3. In relation to so gentle a death as the aforesaid apostle is said to die by, which doth argue a kind of lenity, or mildness in that tyrant, as being but his first entrance into that tragedy, being compared with the cruelties which he is said to use afterward, yea, and that even to his own mother, whose very womb he is said to have caused to be ripped open, to the end he might see the place of his conception, with many other cruelties which are reported of him, all which doth argue the apostle's death (as aforesaid) to have been the first entrance of that tyrant into his butchery of the saints.

I shall in the next place discover the original of the beast which was to act the second part of that Christian tragedy, begun by the aforesaid Nero, and continued during the ten persecutions (viz.) from the aforesaid Claudius Nero, unto Constantius Magnus, in whose days the aforesaid ten persecutions had their period.

Who seeing the aforesaid emperors his predecessors frustrated of their expectation (viz.) of a total extirpation of the primitive church and frame of gospel-government from off the earth, and that notwithstanding all their bloody massacres, and killing courses, whereby many thousands were oft-times slain in a day, resolved to take a more subtle course, and that by practicing another design to the same effect, which was by giving a seat and power, and great authority unto such silly souls as he could by that means delude and ensnare; "To the end he might do that by craft and subtlety, which his predecessors could not do by force and violence." To which purpose I say it doth plainly appear that the said Constantius &c. called the great Council of Nicea, in which Diet the aforesaid Constantius, and they decreed, that like as the King of the Romans was then called Emperor above other Kings, so the Bishop of the same city, should be called Pope, above other Bishops. And to the more specious carrying on of the aforesaid design, he likewise erected many sumptuous temples or churches, decking them with jewels, and costly ornaments; and to the end he might further procure his ends therein, he gave likewise to the priests of them times (whom he had so ensnared under pretence of advancing and promoting religion) worldly power and great riches, that they might more freely manage his design. And to carry it on yet further, he likewise pretended to have seen the sign of the cross in the air, and thereby took occasion to set up imagery and idolatry of crosses,[3] and saints' relics, yea, and what not, which might tend to an Aaronical glory, into which dress he was then determined to transform or reduce the then afflicted church of Jesus Christ; supposing it the only time and means to bring that his purpose to pass. All which and much more, Eusebius and other historians report of him in a plentiful manner; by all which means the cross of Christ began to be made of none effect, and the power of Christ's death either no more remembered, or no more understood by the deluded professors of such false worship. Insomuch, as a voice was then heard from heaven saying, "This day is poison poured forth into the church," all which doth clearly demonstrate the aforesaid Constantius to be the very Man, or Dragon, who gave his power unto the beast, as Rev. 13.

Having thus discovered the place where, the time when, and the manner how the Dragon, and the beast took their first rise, I shall in the next place compute the time of the aforesaid 1260 years, (which was assigned to be the time of the hiding of the primitive church, &c. in its wilderness condition) from the rise of the beast or Papacy, to which purpose, it is very remarkable, that between the birth of Constantius, and the death of Luther, is fully expired the aforesaid number of years, Constantius being born in the year 283, and Luther's death happening in the year, 1546 from which latter number if you deduct, the former, the remainder will be 1263 years as by comparing of Eusebius with Mr. Fox in his Book of Martyrs, upon the life and death of the aforesaid Constantius and Luther will appear: So that it is probable the aforesaid primitive church, &c. came out of its wilderness condition, about three years before the death of Luther.

Now that it came forth as aforesaid, not by the means of Luther, but rather contrary to his desire, will clearly appear by this ensuing story of Spanhemus, professor of Leiden in his Historical Narrative of the Church of Christ in Germany, which that enemy of the truth there styleth, by the scandalous name of Anabaptists, in which story contrary to his intended desire he testifieth the visibility of the aforesaid true church in Luther's

[3]From whence sprung the cross in baptism.

time, as the aforesaid story will clearly manifest,[4] where speaking out of ignorance, by way of contempt against three famous champions of the primitive church of Jesus Christ (which was at that very instant making its first approach out of its wilderness condition, in its morning dress) useth these following expressions, by way of narration, viz.

"That when God raised up Luther, Melanchthon, Zuinglius, and divers other worthies, to be reformers of his church, at the same time the enemy of mankind raised up the Anabaptists to be the disturbers of his church: That Thomas Muntzer their great Antisignanus, &c. when he could not get Luther to join with him, &c. began to thunder against Luther himself, crying out, that Luther was as much in fault as the Pope of Rome, yea, and more, yea, that Luther, and those of his party, savoured nothing but of the flesh, vaunting indeed, that they had cut off some of the leaves of antichrist, but the tree and the root remained still untouched, which (said Muntzer, Storch, and Becold) must be cut down, and which cut down they would."

So that the Papacy, Prelacy, and Presbytery, may fitly be compared to three families under one roof, striving to supplant each other, witness the continual conflicts between the old Strumpet and her aforesaid daughters, and that as it were in a battle royal, both by word and sword, to subvert each other's hierarchies, which they have already done in a great measure in this nation, the full accomplishment whereof I hope in a short time to see effected both in this nation and elsewhere, which the Lord in much mercy hasten, that the truth of his promises may be fulfilled in these our days, which was written by his servant John, Rev. 13. 10 viz. "That such as have and would lead the primitive church of Christ captive, may be led themselves into captivity, and that such as have killed them with the sword, &c. may be killed by the sword," &c. Rev. 18. 6,7,8.

---

[4]Reader, take notice that this story of the Anabaptists (scandalously so called) was written by an utter adversary to the truth, as I shall hereafter make appear. Or otherwise through his ignorance of the truth. Take notice also that the aforesaid champions of the truth, (viz.) Muntzer, &c. appeared at the same time that Luther, &c. began to oppose the Pope, so that when there was but the least way made for the church of Christ to appear, it had its champions to publish it to the world, as by their expressions to Luther did appear, wherein they spoke nothing but the very truth, for without all controversy, Luther, &c. was no other than Romish sectaries, yea, such as made only a division in Rome, but not from Rome, and so consequently, such as was never of the true church of Jesus Christ, and therefore the Papists may boldly, and justly, question the Prelates, where their religion was before Luther, as also the Presbyterians before Calvin, inasmuch as they are no other than the daughters of that grand Harlot, Rev. 17. 5. Witness their national churches, their Popish institution of priests, and baptizing of infants, which are infallible characters, to prove them harlots like their mother.

Psal. 149. 6,7,8,9. and that the true primitive church may be restored to such a latitude, as to spread itself over the face of the whole earth, as in Dan. 7. 18,27.

But to return where I left (viz.) to the first approach of the aforesaid primitive church in its morning's dress, as you yourself have very elegantly described it, page 1, &c. where from Canticles 6.10 you compare the degrees of the approach thereof out of its wilderness condition. 1. To be like the looking forth of the morning. 2. To the fairness of the moon. 3. To the clearness of the sun. And lastly, to the terribleness of an army with banners. All which are indeed most excellent and lively emblems of the degrees which have been, and are yet, to be taken by the aforesaid primitive church, since her wilderness condition.

Which aforesaid gradations, was doubtless the only reason, why the aforesaid Spanhemus, Luther, &c. could not at that time discern the aforesaid church to be the primitive church, which was then looking, or peeping out of its wilderness condition; and that inasmuch also, because of the long hiding thereof (viz.) for the aforesaid space of 1260 years, during which time of its absence, it was departed from them, as it had been into another world (as your self doth also acknowledge) so that they were in the interim set down in darkness, and so knew not the aforesaid true church at that time of the approach thereof, but continued rather wondering at it, and hating it, &c. (which is now your own present condition, which I humbly desire you would lay to heart, by a serious consideration of your present estate, and to redeem the time you have hitherto spent in deluding, and being deluded, which phrase I am constrained to use, hoping it may be unto you, as such a reproof as the prophet David desireth to be reproved by, Psal. 141. 5 which he there esteemeth, as a precious balm upon his head).

At...

It is at this point that page 16 in the original ends, with the first word (i.e. "At") of page 17 appearing at the bottom right-hand corner. The text resumes in the original with a broken word on page 21, which now follows.

...-cover their ordination (unto you) by the constitution of their church.

Now they cannot avoid, but that the constitution of their church, is now the same with that party, or church, which did separate from the Papacy of that time, from which they derive their succession. So that if the constitution (and so consequently the ordination) of the now Presbyterian churches and ministers be constituted and ordained contrary to the command of Jesus Christ, and the practice of his apostles: then it must unavoidably follow, that the aforesaid party which Mr. Cranford saith, did so separate themselves from the Papacy, was also constituted and ordained contrary to the commands of Jesus Christ, and the practice of his apostles.

But that the present church whereof Mr. Cranford is now termed the minister, &c. is a church constituted (and so consequently ordained) contrary to the command of Jesus Christ, and the practice of his apostles I thus argue.

That church which is constituted of such persons as have neither been taught, nor have faith, repentance, baptism, is a church constituted contrary to the commands of Jesus Christ, and the practice of his apostles. Mat. 28. 19,20. Mark 16. 15,16. Acts 2. 38,41. and 8. 12,35,36. &c. and 16. 14,15,31,32,33.

But the aforesaid church, whereof Mr. Cranford is minister, &c. hath been so constituted as aforesaid, viz. of infants sprinkled, &c.

Ergo, the aforesaid church whereof Mr. Cranford is minister, is constituted contrary to the command of Jesus Christ, and the practice of his apostles.

2. That church which is constituted contrary to the commands of Jesus Christ, and the practice of his apostles, is no constituted church of Jesus Christ.

But the aforesaid church of Mr. Cranford's hath been so constituted. Ergo it is no constituted church of Jesus Christ.

3. That church which is not a constituted church of Jesus Christ, is a constituted church of antichrist.

But the aforesaid church of Mr. Cranford is not a constituted church of Jesus Christ, &c.

Ergo it is a constituted church of antichrist.

4. That church which is a constituted church of antichrist, is a church constituted by the power and authority of antichrist.

But Mr. Cranford's church is a constituted church of antichrist:

Ergo constituted by the authority and power of antichrist.

5. That church which is constituted by the power and authority of antichrist, is one and the same with antichrist *in its constitution,* &c.

But Mr. Cranford's church as aforesaid, is constituted by the authority and power of antichrist:

Ergo it is one and the same with antichrist in its constitution, &c.

6. That church, whose constitution is one and the same with the

church of antichrist in its constitution, is not separated from the constitution of the antichristian church.

But the constitution of Mr. Cranford's church, &c. is one and the same with the constitution of the church of antichrist.

Ergo the constitution of Mr. Cranford's church was never separated from the constitution of the church of antichrist, and so consequently, neither that party, or church, formerly instanced by Mr. Cranford, from whom he, and the whole Presbyterian party, do plead succession from, as to their constitution and ordination, and so consequently, all such as plead the like succession and ordination as they do.

For that church, whose constitution is antichristian, cannot ordain ministers of Jesus Christ.

But the constitution of the aforesaid churches is antichristian, ergo, they cannot ordain ministers of Jesus Christ.

So that all the churches that have been constituted by baptizing or sprinkling of infants, as aforesaid, have been constituted by the authority and power of antichrist.

But all the aforesaid churches who pretend to have been separated from antichrist, did never separate from the constitution of the church of antichrist.

Ergo, the constitution of all the aforesaid churches have continued antichristian, from their separation to this present, and so consequently have neither had a true constitution or ordination, as the churches or ministers of Jesus Christ, since their aforesaid separation.

But to leave them without any further plea in this particular, I shall urge the writings of them, whom they so highly esteem as the great reformers of their times, presuming the testimony that they shall afford to my present purpose will be of force to leave an impress upon their consciences. I shall begin with Melanchthon, who in his Answer to the Anabaptists is enforced to confess,[5] that about the year of our Lord 248, and after the departure of John the oldest apostle, 158 years, there lived a certain priest one Fidus, who would that men should according to the manner of circumcision baptize young children upon the eighth day, with whom saith he, Cyprian[6] with 66 Bishops and Elders more gathered together joined themselves and ordained, that everyone without delay should receive baptism, and that young children should be timely brought thereunto; after which (saith Bullinger) the Carthaginian Council concluded thus to Innocentius, viz.[7]

---

[5]The marginal reference is covered by what looks to be a piece of tape.

[6]Note the power of antichrist in the year, 248

[7]Bullingerus ex Augustino contra Julianum, lib. 1. cap. 2.

"Forasmuch as we believe that Christ the Son of God was holily born of the pure Virgin Mary to fulfill and ratify the promises of God, which excludeth not children from salvation, we will therefore that they be baptized."

In which two instances we have the grand foundation laid to the mystery of iniquity (foretold by the apostle Paul, 2 Thes. 2. 1,2,3,4, &c. as also by John 1 epist. 2.18,19) whereupon antichrist was to erect his fabric apart from the true church, from which they had revolted, (as in the aforesaid Scriptures) and that chiefly instead of circumcision, upon which basis it is yet supported by the daughters of the aforesaid Harlot, the original of the rise thereof, being like[8] unto that of Jeroboam the son of Nebat, who when he had through his subtlety procured a revolt of the ten tribes from their obedience to the house of David, 1 King. 12. And after considering what would be the event thereof, if he should not use some means to bottom their worship apart from each other (as in v. 26, 27, 28, &c) did thereupon take counsel, &c. By means whereof he erected another foundation to settle the aforesaid revolters upon, by way of allusion to what they had formerly practiced; by which his subtlety, he is said to continue a firm and sure separation of the aforesaid revolters from those of their brethren, that kept themselves to their first principle of obedience and loyalty to the aforesaid house of David, &c. So in like manner when the aforesaid[9] revolters from the truth were grown so numerous as aforesaid, they thought it high time to use the like craft and subtlety, as the aforesaid Jeroboam did, to the end their like rebellious consorts or renigados should not return to their former faith, or worship; and hence it was that they also took counsel together as aforesaid, where they likewise concluded, that instead of their former constitution founded upon baptizing of such as had been taught, believed, and repented, as hath been clearly proved, they should now constitute their churches, by baptizing of infants, without any reference to the aforesaid motives, (viz.) of being taught, or having faith or repentance, by which means their church became every whit as distinct, or separate from the church of Jesus Christ, as the aforesaid revolting Israelites became to the house of David. But lest Mr. Cranford, &c. should say these are my own words, without any further testimony, to strengthen and confirm the same, in point of history, or human testimony, I shall therefore present you with the opinions and judgments of such, who albeit[10] enemies to the true baptism of the true church, as their practice did declare, yet being urged

[8]Simile, The revolt of antichrist compared with the revolt of the ten tribes from the house of David.

[9]Viz. Fallers from the faith, 2 Thes. 2. 3. 1 John -?- Pray read these texts. The chapter and verse for 1 John are obliterated in the margin in the original.

[10]The enemies of the truth forced to speak contrary to their own practice.

to speak their consciences in relation thereunto, have declared and published as followeth. And first of the confession of[11] Luther himself, who in his book entitled, The Ground-Work and Cause, Tom. 1 where speaking of the sacraments, useth these expressions upon the words of Jesus Christ, Mark 16. 16 (viz.) "That these words are spoken in reference to faith before baptism, concluding that where faith is not, there baptism[12] availeth not," as the following words of the same place doth show, saying, "He that believeth not shall be damned, &c. For it is not baptism, but by faith in baptism that saveth," as we read Acts 8. 36: "That Philip would not baptize the eunuch until he had first demanded of him, whether he believed, &c. But without faith the sacraments profit nothing; yea, they are not only in vain, but bring damnation also to the receivers."

Again, writing upon the 48th chapter of Genesis, he saith, "That before we receive the sacrament of baptism, and the Lord's Supper, we must have faith."

Again, in his book of the Civil Magistrate he also saith, "That the sacrament neither can, nor may be received without faith[13] but with great hurt, &c. So that either before, or else even then present, when baptism is administered, there must needs be faith, or else there is a contempt of the divine Majesty, who offers his present grace when there is none to receive it."

Again, in his Epistle of Anabaptism, he confesseth, "That it cannot be proved by any place of Scripture, that children do believe, neither do the Scriptures clearly or plainly with these or the like words say, baptize your children,[14] for they believe: wherefore we must yield to those that drive us to the letter, because we find it nowhere written."

Melancht.[15] on 1 Cor. 11 saith,[16] "In times past, those that had repented then were baptized, and was instead of an absolution, wherefore repentance must not be separate from baptism, for baptism is a sacramental sign of repentance."

Again, in his treatise concerning the Doctrine of Anabaptists, he is forced to confess, "that there is[17] no plain commandment in the holy Scriptures, that children should be baptized."

---

[11]The testimony of Luther.

[12]What then availeth infant sprinkling?

[13]Marginal reference obliterated by what appears to be a piece of tape.

[14]But if unbelievers, then why are they baptized?

[15]The testimony of Melanchthon.

[16]Note.

[17]How then dare they do it, contrary to the practice of the apostles?

Zuinglius[18] in his book saith, "That[19] in old time children were openly instructed, who when they came to understanding were called chatecumeni, that is, such as are instructed in the word of salvation; and when they had imprinted the faith in their hearts, and made confession thereof with their mouths, they were admitted to baptism."

Again, in his book of the Movers of Sedition he likewise useth this expression, viz. "When we speak of children's baptism, so it is, that there is no plain word in the Scriptures, whereby the same is commanded."

Calvin[20] likewise is put to confess, "That it is nowhere expressly mentioned by the Evangelists, that any one child was by the[21] apostles' hands baptized."

Having thus given you the testimonies of the late great pretended reformers, &c. (though contrary to their practice) I shall in the next place give you the like testimonies of other writers relating to baptism, as it was practiced in the apostles' days, and the first two hundred years after.

Hier.[22] saith, "The Lord commanded his apostles, that they should first instruct and teach all nations, and[23] afterwards should baptize those that were instructed in the mysteries of faith," &c.

Athan.[24] saith, "That our Saviour did not slightly command to baptize, but first of all he said, teach, and then baptize, that true faith might come by teaching, and baptism be perfected by faith."

Haimo[25] saith, "That there is set down a rule[26] rightly how to baptize, that is, that teaching should go before baptism, for he saith, teach all nations, and then he saith, baptize them, for he that is to be baptized must be before instructed, that he first learn to believe that which in baptism he shall receive; for as faith without works is dead, so works when they are not of faith are nothing worth."

Roffensis[27] saith, "The now rulers of churches use such baptism as Christ never used in his church."

---

[18]The testimony of Zuinglius. Art. 18.

[19]Note old time, and why not so now?

[20]The testimony of Calvin in his Institutions, lib. 4. cap. 16.

[21]If not by the apostles, by whom then I pray?

[22]The testimony of Hieronymus upon Mat. 28. 19,20.

[23]Then not before.

[24]The testimony of Athanatius, in his third sermon against the Arians. Idem.

[25]Item Haimo in Postilla, fol. 278. Idem.

[26]If such be right baptism, then the other is wrong.

[27]Roffensis contra cap. Balilon.

Eck[28] writing against the new church orders, &c. saith, "That the ordinance concerning the baptism of children is without Scripture," and concludes thus against the Lutherans; "What are you such fools, to take on you the ordinances of men, which is found only to be a custom of the church?"

Orig.[29] calls baptism of children,[30] "a ceremony and tradition of the church," in Levit. Hom. 8 in Epist. ad Rom. lib. 5. Augustine[31] also calleth it "a custom of the church," De Baptismo contra Donat. lib. 4. cap. 23. Pope Gregory[32] calleth it, "a tradition of the Fathers," in Decretis Destinet de Consecrat. Cassander, in his book De Infantum Baptismo, saith, "That it came to be used by the Fathers which lived three hundred years after Christ."[33]

From all which it is clearly proved (and that from the mouths of such as did then practice infant-baptism or sprinkling) that all such persons as have been incorporated into church-fellowship by being baptized or sprinkled, while infants were incorporated by a way or means that Jesus Christ never commanded to be used to such a purpose, as also by such a way as was never practiced by his apostles, and so consequently not incorporated visible members of the church of Jesus Christ, but contrariwise, visible members of the visible church of antichrist, whose invention it was, and whose practice it yet is, instance Mr. Cranford's church as aforesaid, and therefore as antichristian as the rest; and so consequently the ordination, which Mr. Cranford and the rest of the ministers of London (Presbyterian ministers) have received, from such as have been so baptized or sprinkled as aforesaid, is every whit as antichristian as their baptism, which hath been clearly made out to be a mere tradition of men, and therefore abominable in the church of Jesus Christ, Mat. 15. 8.

Having thus clearly proved, that all the aforesaid societies of people, are neither churches or ministers of Jesus Christ (albeit their separations as aforesaid) it must of necessity follow, that the church, or society of people (now scandalously termed Anabaptists) was ever kept distinct and separate from antichrist, and that to all ends and purposes whatsoever, whether in essentials, substantials, and circumstantials, so that the aforesaid primitive church and frame of gospel-government, was never

[28]Doctor Eckius a popish priest in Enchiridion.

[29]Origen.

[30]Then a Pharisaical manner of worship.

[31]Augustine.

[32]Pope Gregory.

[33]Cassander. He guessed within 52 years.

totally destroyed in her externals by the aforesaid red Dragon, or beast, or antichrist (maugre all their malice and endeavours to do the same) much less in her internals, but contrariwise preserved and continued unto this present time; and therefore it will be needless to answer your third assertion,viz.

"That the gospel-frame of gospel-government is to be restored by some one man," &c.

For what need is there of restoring that by any one man, when the aforesaid church hath power to do it (when need requireth) of, and by itself, the church of Christ being as a tree (Psal. 1. 3) whose seed is in itself: now experience teacheth us, that a tree so planted as aforesaid, albeit in the autumnal or winter season, it becomes seemingly dead, by being deprived of its outward ornaments of leaves and fruit (which is procured by the coldness of the season, which causeth the sap to shrink down into the root) yet the like experience doth also teach us, that at the springtime, the aforesaid sap or moisture, being exhaled again by virtue of the heat of the sun, doth furnish the same tree again with its like natural ornaments of leaves and fruit, and that of, and from itself.

So put the case, that during the autumnal or winter season of the antichristian persecution of the church of Christ, it might be deprived of its aforesaid ornaments of order, and form of worship, yet the root and the tree being preserved (viz. the word of God as the root, and saints as the tree, wherein the aforesaid order and form of worship have been retained, during the aforesaid time) hath by the virtue and power of the Sun of righteousness shining upon it (at the time of its approach out of its aforesaid condition) even as much power to furnish itself with its spiritual ornaments, of order, and form of worship, and that without any other artificial help whatsoever, as the aforesaid tree hath to produce its own leaves and fruit.

But lest what hath been said shall not satisfy you, I shall answer the particulars, wherein you conceive it defective, as first in point of its present constitution, and ordination.

In answer to which I shall refer you to the commands and practices of Jesus Christ, and his apostles, relating to the constitution and ordination of the church which they first gathered, as in Mat. 28. 18,19,20. Mark 16. 15,16,17. As also the book of the Acts, viz. by teaching, and baptizing, in the gatherers, as also by faith, repentance, and being baptized, in such as were gathered thereunto, which hath been, and is yet, the present practice of those that have and do yet succeed the apostles in that gospel-church so gathered by them, viz. the church now scandalously termed Anabaptists: And therefore one and the same with the aforesaid gospel-church so gathered as aforesaid.

Object. But you will reply, that the standing officers in the primitive church, ceased, while it was in its wilderness condition.

Answ. What need of deacons was there in the church at Jerusalem before the number of the disciples were multiplied, Acts 6. 1. &c. or when the aforesaid church was scattered abroad by the then persecution, (viz.) the whole church, "except the apostles," Acts 8. 1? And yet I presume you will not deny there was a church of Jesus Christ then at Jerusalem, as in Acts 8. 14.

So likewise when the aforesaid primitive church, was penned up into mountains, dens, deserts, and caves of the earth, and when, as it is likely, not above eight or ten persons might meet in one place together, what need had they of evangelists, pastors, teachers, elders, deacons, &c. when one or two of them might supply the place of them all (so far as there was need of them) and so likewise in relation to the rest of the ordinances, what need was there of any other than of private teachings, prophesying, prayer, baptism, breaking of bread, which I have fully cleared to all rational men, might be then performed by the aforesaid church in its then condition, where I compared it with the present condition of the Popish synagogue in this nation: And without which it had been impossible it should have subsisted for so long a time as 1260 years, (which that it did, I have also cleared by the aforesaid instances of Muntzer, Storch, and Becold, in their addresses to Luther, when the aforesaid time was expired), albeit the said Luther was ignorant thereof, supposing (as yet you do) that the aforesaid primitive church had been devolved into the then antichristian estate, of which he then conceived himself a reformer, (the contrary to which I think I have clearly proved) however I am confident, that the then poor distressed saints, had as much respect to observe all the commands of Jesus Christ, as possibly were then in their power to prosecute, during their aforesaid wilderness condition, in the aforesaid mountains, dens, deserts, and caves of the earth, whereunto they were confined, and in which they were preserved.

Object. Peradventure you will bid me prove that the aforesaid primitive church was so preserved, and where.

Answ. It is enough for me to prove that it was only to be hid, and so hid from the face of the Dragon, &c. As that the said Dragon, &c. could not find it, or make discovery of it, which is your own confession, pag. 2 in your aforesaid book: By which your expressions it is evident, 1. That it was only to be hid. Ergo, it had a being where it was so hid. 2. You say it was hid from the Dragon, &c. Ergo, not devolved into the Dragon, &c. 3. You say the Dragon could not find it, or make discovery of it. Ergo, it was apart from him, or otherwise such words were ridiculous.

But that you declare the very truth in so saying, (though not wittingly)[34] I shall prove further from Scripture, where Jesus Christ promiseth to be with it to the end of the world, Matth. 28. 20. Ergo, it was to have a continuance unto the end of the world. And if so, then during the aforesaid time of 1260 years. Again, if continued a church, then in all the essentials, substantials, and circumstantials that appertained unto it, (so far as there was need of, in its then condition) as aforesaid. Again, I would gladly know any one church (in that which we now call Christendom) that can produce the like hidden condition,[35] as the church now scandalously termed Anabaptists. And much more in that it is so clearly discovered to be so near, yea even one and the same with the pattern of the first church that was erected by the commands of Jesus Christ, and the practice of the apostles. And as to the place where it was so preserved, it may be probably conjectured to be in Germany,[36] inasmuch as the aforesaid Muntzer, &c. did there discover themselves at the time aforesaid.

Redeem the time therefore which you have hitherto spent in opposing so plain a truth (as hath been declared) by disclaiming that error, as you have done many more, (viz. your sprinkling and ordination, &c.) in doing of which, you will have the benefit, I my desire, and God the glory.

FINIS

You may have this book, as also another lately published by John More (entitled, A General Exhortation to the World, &c.) at the Shop of Giles Calvert at the Black Spread-Eagle at the West End of Paul's.

[34]Many speak truth though not wittingly or willingly.

[35]Neither the Popish, Prelatical, Presbyterian, &c. churches can claim the like hidden state and condition, as &c.

[36]Germany the most probable place of the church's hiding, &c.